SHOTOKAN KARATE

5th kyu to Black Be'

Sensei K Enoeda · 8th Dan

A & C Black · London

First published 1996 by
A & C Black (Publishers) Ltd
35 Bedford Row, London WC1R 4JH

Copyright © 1996 by Tiger Corporation

ISBN 0 7136 4312 9

A CIP catalogue record for this book
is available from the British Library.

Printed and bound in Great Britain by
Hillman Printers Ltd, Frome, Somerset

Acknowledgements
Written by Jim Lewis 5th Dan.
Thanks to Steve Smith 3rd Dan, Rod
Butler 3rd Dan, Chieko Buck.
Sensei Enoeda's assistants: Sensei Y. Ohta
5th Dan, Sensei J. Lewis 5th Dan.

Back cover photograph by Adrian Nessel.
All other photography by Sylvio Dokov.

Disclaimer
Whilst every effort has been made to
ensure accuracy within this book, the
writer and his publisher cannot accept
any responsibility for accident or injury
caused through misinterpretation of its
contents. The reader is urged to use the
book as a complement to regular training
with a qualified instructor.

Contents

Introduction

To the tens of thousands of students throughout the world who are already practising karate-ka, the names **Shotokan** and **Keinosuke Enoeda** are synonymous.

A history of Shotokan karate and the Japan Karate Association

The late 1970s and early 1980s saw a great explosion of interest in the martial arts, the effects of which continue to this day. The result is a multitude of styles and organisations, some of which have developed and prospered while others have declined and disappeared. One style which has grown to become one of the most widely taught is Shotokan as practised by the Japan Karate Association (JKA). Formed in 1955, the JKA is now the world's largest Shotokan karate organisation, with affiliated members in almost every country throughout the world. Great Britain is affiliated through the Karate Union of Great Britain (KUGB).

To trace the origin of karate we have to go back over a thousand years to ancient China, to the monastery at Shao Lin. Here the students were taught the art of fighting as part of their spiritual and religious training, and as a way of building strength and character.

These fighting techniques were later imported to Okinawa where the feudal Lord of that time had banned the carrying and use of weapons. These Chinese techniques combined with the local fighting techniques of the islands to form a self-defence fighting system which developed into what we know today as karate.

Gichin Funakoshi

One master of these fighting arts was **Gichin Funakoshi,** considered to be the founder of the modern day Shotokan style. Originally from the island of Okinawa (where he had studied various forms of martial arts), he first introduced the style to Japan in 1922. There he opened his first dojo (training hall) in 1936. 'Shoto' was his nickname; hence the name **Shoto kan** – Shoto's house or hall.

Master Funakoshi died at the age of 87 in 1957 but not before he had witnessed the inception of what was to produce, through the now famous JKA instructor training programme, some of the finest karate instructors in the world.

Keinosuke Enoeda

Among that élite group of early instructors was Master Keinosuke Enoeda, the 'Tiger' of whom so much has already been written. Born in 1935 a direct descendant of two Samurai lines, he first began studying judo and attained the rank of second degree Black Belt. At the age of 15 he began studying karate under Master Gichin Funakoshi and Masatoshi Nakayama, who was later to become the Chief Instructor of the JKA.

After graduating from university in 1957, he was invited to enroll on the three-year instructor's course at the JKA. It was during this time that he became All-Japan Champion, earning the nickname 'Tiger' for his exceptional fighting spirit. He is also credited with possessing the strongest punch in all of Japan, a result of his tremendous technique and constant practice on the makiwara (striking board).

On completion of the instructor course, Master Enoeda travelled the world for several years teaching karate, eventually settling in Great Britain. Here he made his home and here he has remained for the past 30 years as the Chief Instructor of the KUGB. It is without doubt that through his unique training and teaching ability, much admired and respected by instructors and students everywhere, Master Enoeda has been a leading figure in making Great Britain one of the strongest karate countries in the world. Master Enoeda continues to teach at his own dojo, and throughout the world where his spirit and dedication to karate are as much a source of inspiration as they were 30 years ago.

Together, the two volumes in the Shotokan karate series will guide the student from beginner right through to Black Belt, with expert guidance, from one of the world's most dynamic karate instructors. I have been a student of Sensei Enoeda for over 25 years, and I was very proud to be asked to contribute to this series which I know will not only delight, but become an invaluable source of reference to all Shotokan karate students whether they are already training or are just about to start.

Both volumes are designed to provide a comprehensive textbook covering each 'grade' (level of advancement) through which the student will be required to progress. However, it must be stressed that no amount of text or number of photographs can compensate for regular training. Only through constant practice will the student become proficient and excel at karate.

If this approach is adopted and a regular training programme adhered to, the rewards will be very worthwhile.

In this the second of our two book series, Sensei Enoeda will guide you through the syllabus covering the grades 5th kyu (Purple Belt) to the coveted Black Belt. This book will enable students to graft on to their existing range of karate techniques the more exacting variations that he or she will require for a steady progression through the grading levels.

As with our previous volume, katas are explained in both words and pictures so that each move can be studied by the student and a truly accurate representation of every kata can be performed.

As you progress through the book, learning more and more, perhaps you might reflect that even skills already learned need to be practised: a mark of the great instructors is their ability never to tire of practising their basic technique.

Finally, should you complete the course and attain the Black Belt there will be a recognition that, far from being the end of learning, it is in fact just the beginning.

Karate as exercise

It is worthwhile remembering that karate practice is an ideal way to promote a healthier lifestyle. The exercises involve the use of the whole body, enhancing flexibility, muscle strength and stamina to develop a well balanced body.

Karate can be practised alone or in a class group, it does not require a partner, or any special equipment or apparatus, and can be practised just about anywhere. It is suitable for men and women of all ages, and as a 'kata', for example, takes about two minutes to perform, it does not require a huge amount of time. Regular training can help to build character and discipline as well as self-confidence.

Karate, however, is much more than just physical exercise. Karate requires a positive mental attitude allied with appropriate etiquette, which should be adopted both in and out of the dojo. Always maintain a courteous and respectful attitude not only towards your teacher and fellow students, but also towards everyone you come into contact with.

This positive mental attitude is best illustrated as follows. At the end of each lesson the whole class adopts a kneeling position and after a few moments silence all the students together repeat the following.

Dojo code (*See* artwork on page 8.)
• Seek perfection of character.
• Be faithful.
• Endeavour.
• Respect others.
• Refrain from violent behaviour.

These five tenets should form the basis not only of your karate practice, but also your attitude to everyday life. As you progress through your karate training you will begin to realise the importance of a correct mental attitude.

I would like to say a special thank you to Sensei Yoshinabu Ohta, 5th Dan JKA, for all his help in putting together this series and for demonstrating his superb techniques. Sensei Ohta is a graduate of the famous Takushoku University, Japan. He was placed third in kata in the 1986 All-Japan Karate Championships, and has been Sensei Enoeda's assistant since 1982. Without his invaluable aid these books would not have been possible.

Finally, I would like to convey some of my own personal experiences in over 25 years in karate. During that time I have been most fortunate in being taught by some of the finest instructors in the world, some of whom have now become good friends.

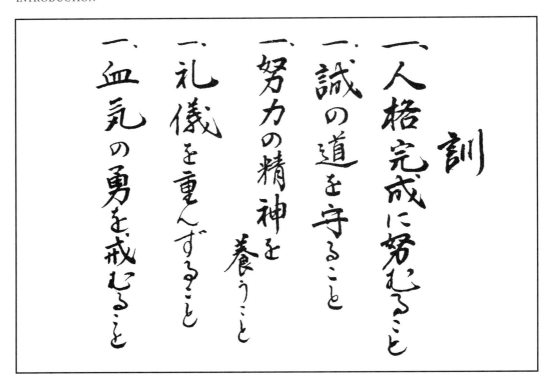

訓

一、人格完成に努むること

一、誠の道を守ること

一、努力の精神を養うこと

一、礼儀を重んずること

一、血気の勇を戒むること

　Some students who started out with me and are now themselves instructors have also become close personal friends, and have been very helpful in putting together this series. I would like to particularly thank Mr Steve Smith, 3rd Dan, for his invaluable comments and criticisms.

　Wherever I have travelled in the world, I have always found a local dojo where I have without exception been made extremely welcome, and where I have met some fascinating and interesting people. One such trip to Thailand in 1988 led me to be appointed the Head Coach to the Thai National Karate Team, representing Thailand at the South East Asian Games in Kualar Lumpar in 1989. Over the years karate has enabled me to be involved in many such opportunities, and I hope that those of you who are starting out on your karate training will find it as rewarding and enriching as I have.

Jim Lewis 5th Dan

Master Enoeda's dojo is located at: 16 Marshall Street, London W1V 1LN (tel 0171-734-0900).

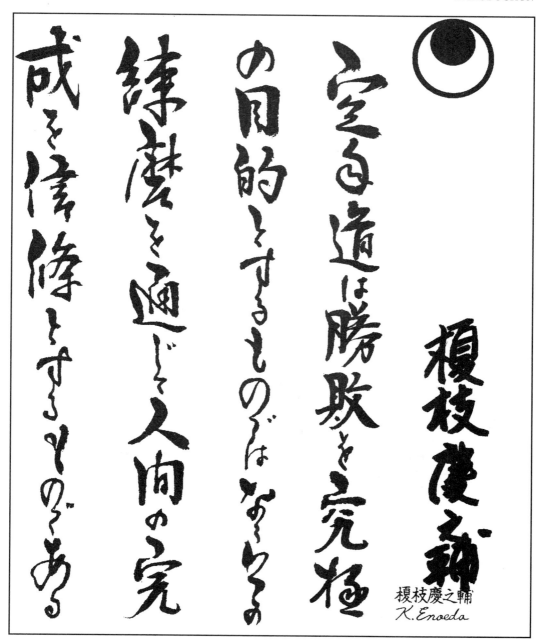

空手道は勝敗を完福の目的とするものではなく練磨を通じて人間の完成を信條とするものである

榎枝慶之輔
K. Enoeda

The ultimate aim of the art of karate lies not in victory or defeat, but in the perfection of the characters of its participants.

Gichin Funakoshi

9

Each book is divided into separate levels for each grade, and each level covers **kihon – kata – kumite**.

Volume one: 10th kyu to 6th kyu
Level one: 9th kyu
Level two: 8th kyu
Level three: 7th kyu
Level four: 6th kyu

Volume two: 5th kyu to Black Belt
Level five: 5th kyu
Level six: 4th kyu
Level seven: 3rd kyu
Level eight: 2nd kyu
Level nine: 1st kyu
Level ten: shodan 1st Dan

Warm-up

Before you begin your karate practice or any type of strenuous exercise, it is important to thoroughly warm up the whole body through a series of gentle movements and stretches. This prepares the body for the actual karate movements.

Grading

Shotokan karate has a system of grades or levels of competence (kyu) from 10th kyu (beginner) to 1st kyu. The next level up from 1st kyu is Black Belt or shodan (1st Dan). When a student reaches a certain level of proficiency, he or she may try for a grading (assessment) and if successful the student is entitled to wear a coloured belt which denotes the grade attained. These are:

10th kyu – White Belt
9th kyu – Orange Belt
8th kyu – Red Belt
7th kyu – Yellow Belt
6th kyu – Green Belt
5th kyu – Purple Belt
4th kyu – Purple Belt
3rd kyu – Brown Belt
2nd kyu – Brown Belt
1st kyu – Brown Belt
1st Dan – Black Belt.

Each grade consists of three elements: **kihon** (basic techniques); **kata**; **kumite** (sparring). Before a student can try for a grade he or she will have to be proficient in all three elements relevant to the grade they are taking.

Kata

To fully explain all the principles involved in the meaning of kata would take a complete book on its own! This is not the purpose of this series. Much has already been written on the subject of kata; the student would be advised to seek out these publications for a more detailed understanding.

Put in its most simplistic form, kata is a series of pre-arranged movements of defence and attack, performed in a specific sequence against one or more imaginary opponents. In earlier times kata was used as a means of teaching technique. When techniques were shown in pre-arranged sequences they could be remembered and practised.

Kata involves the use of all the techniques found in karate: punch, strike, kick, evade, balance, jump, the correct use of power, speed, co-ordination, breathing and timing. All these elements are used and brought together in kata practice.

Daily practice in kata will not only help the student to improve his or her technique, but will also assist in learning the true meaning of karate.

The Shotokan style as shown in this series has a total of 27 katas. For our purposes, however, this series covers only eight of those required to Black Belt. They are:

(1) kihon
(2) heian shodan
(3) heian nidan
(4) heian sandan
(5) heian yondan
(6) heian godan
(7) tekki shodan
(8) bassai dai.

Note   Within each of the kata sections the counts are indicated by ❶, ❷, ❸, etc.

Level five (5th kyu)

Kihon

Fig.13 *Mawashigeri* (roundhouse kick).
Shows the position for a roundhouse
kick. From front stance lift the knee to
the side and make a round kick.

Side view

Fig.13

Side view

Fig.13

Side view

Fig.13

Side view

15

Fig.13

Side view

Side view

Fig.14 *Shutouchi* (knife hand strike). Shows two ways to make a knife hand strike: (1) with the striking arm pulled back and above the shoulder;

(2) with the striking arm from above the opposite shoulder.

Kata: heian yondan

Fig.1 *Yoi* (ready).

Fig.2 *Haiwanuke*. Step with your left foot to back stance. Make a double hand block.

❶

23

Fig.3 Turn to your opposite direction. Make a back stance double hand block.

❷

24

Fig.4 *Gedankosauke*. Step to your left and make a double hand downward crossing block.

❸

25

Fig.5 *Moroteuke.* Step forward in back stance. Make a right hand block with your left fist to your right elbow.

❹

Fig.6 Left arm: *Urakenuchi;* right arm: *Yokokeage.* Make a side snap kick and back fist strike to your left side.

❺

❻

27

❼

Fig.7 Step to front stance and make a right elbow strike.

Fig.8 Move your left foot halfway to your right foot, turn to your opposite direction and make a side snap kick with your right foot and a back fist strike with your right hand.

Fig.8

❽

❾

Fig.9 Step to front stance and make a left elbow strike. ⑩

Fig.10 Left arm: *Gedan jodan shutouke*; right arm: *Shutouchi*. Make a knife hand downward block with your left hand.

Fig.11 Make a knife hand strike with your right hand, and left hand block.

31

Fig.12 *Jodan Maegeri.* Make a front snap kick to the face with your right foot.

⓭
Fig.13 *Urakenuchi*. Step forward and make an open hand downward pressing block and back fist strike with your right hand with *Kiai*.

Side view

Fig.14 *Kakiwakeuke.*
Move your left foot to
your rear and make a 45°
back stance double hand
block.

Side view

Fig.14

Side view

Fig.15 Make a front snap kick to the face with your right foot.

Side view

Fig.16 Step forward and make a punch with your right hand.

Side view

Fig.17 Make a punch with your left hand.

Side view

Fig.18 Move your right foot to your right, make a back stance to 45° and make a double hand block.

Side view   Side view

39

Fig.19 Make a front snap kick to the face with your left foot.

Side view

Fig.20 Make a stepping punch with your left hand.

Side view

Fig.21 Make a punch with your right hand.

Side view

Fig.22 *Moroteuke*. Move your left foot to your left, make a block with your left hand with your right fist to your left elbow.

Side view

43

Fig.23 Step forward and make a back stance block with your right hand, with the left fist to your right elbow.

㉓

Side view

Fig.24 Step forward and make a back stance block with your left hand, with the right fist to your left elbow.

Side view

45

Fig.25 *Hizatsuchi*. Move your weight to your left foot, open both hands to make knee strike with *Kiai*, pulling both hands downwards as if pulling your opponent's head to your knee.

Side view

Fig.25

Side view

Fig.26 Pivot on your left foot and step down to make a knife hand block with your left hand.

Side view

Fig.26

Side view

Side view

Fig.27 Step forward and make a knife hand block with your right hand.

Fig.28 *Naore.* Step back with your right foot to ready position.

Application

Figs 29, 30, 31, 32 and 33 show the application of figs 10 to 13.　　　　**Fig.29**

Fig.30

Fig.31

Fig.32

Fig.33

Kumite: one-step sparring

As in Level four, but to
include side thrust kick.

Level six (4th kyu)

Kihon

As in Level five.

Kata: heian godan

Kata: heian godan

平安
五段

Fig.1 *Yoi* (ready).

❶
Fig.2 Step with your left foot and make a back stance inside block with your left hand.

56

Fig.3 *Gyakuzuki*. Make a straight punch with your right hand.

❸
Fig.4 *Mizunagarenokamae*. Move your right foot to your left foot, and move your left arm to a position in front of your chest.

❹
Fig.5 Move your right foot and make a back stance inside block with your right hand.

❺
Fig.6 Make a reverse punch with your left hand.

❻
Fig.7 Move your left foot to your right foot and move your right hand to a position in front of your chest as in fig.4.

❼
Fig.8 Step forward with your right foot and make a back stance block with your right hand. Left fist moves to right elbow.

❽
Fig.9 *Gedankosauke*. Step forward and make a double hand downward crossing block.

❾
Fig.10 *Jodan kosaeuke*. Pull back your hands and make an open hand upper double hand crossing block.

❿

Fig.11 *Osaeuke*. Twist your wrist and pull both hands down to a position in front of your left hip.

⓫

Fig.12 Make a left hand punch to your opponent's mid-section.

Fig.13 Make a stepping punch with your right hand with *Kiai*.

⑫

63

Fig.14 Move your right foot to your rear and make a straddle stance downward block with your right hand.

Side view

Fig.14

Side view

Fig.15 *Kakeuke*. Cross your arms and make an open hand block with your left hand.

⓮

⑮
Fig.16 *Mikazuki geri.* With your right foot make a crescent kick to your left hand.

⑯
Fig.17 Step to straddle stance and make an elbow strike with your right hand.

⑰
Fig.18 Pull your left foot behind your right foot. Make a right hand block with your left fist to your right elbow.

Side view

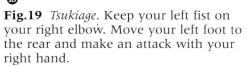

Fig.19 *Tsukiage*. Keep your left fist on your right elbow. Move your left foot to the rear and make an attack with your right hand.

Fig.20 *Gedankosauke*. Jump 180° and make a double hand crossing block with *Kiai*.

⑲

Fig.21 Step with your right foot to your right. Make a block with your right hand, with your left fist to your right elbow.

Side view

Fig.22 Left arm: *Nagashiuke*; right arm: *Shutouchikomi*. Move your left foot and turn to your rear. Make an open hand block with your left hand and a downward attack with your right hand.

㉑

Fig.23 Left arm: *Gedanuke*; right arm: *Jodanuchiuke*. Move your left foot to back stance. Make a downward block with your left hand and an upper inside block with your right hand.

❷
Fig.24 *Heisokudachi.*
Move your left foot and
your right foot together.

Fig.25 Turn and step forward with your right foot.
Make an open hand block with your right hand and a
downward strike with your left hand.

Fig.27 *Naore.* Move your right foot back to ready position.

②

Fig.26 Move your right foot to back stance. Make a downward block with your right hand and an upper inside block with your left hand.

Application

Figs 28, 29, 30, 31 and 32 show the application of figs 9 to 13.

Fig.28

Fig.29

Fig.30

Fig.31

Fig.32

Kumite: one-step sparring

As in Level five.

Level seven (3rd kyu)

Kihon

Fig.15 *Ushirogeri* (back kick). Shows the position for a back kick. From front stance, pivot on the front foot to bring the knee round and up to your supporting leg. Thrust the foot straight out and make a back kick.

Side view

Side view

Side view

Side view

Side view

Kata: tekki shodan

鉄騎初段

Fig.1 *Yoi* (ready). Move your right foot to your left, and place your left hand over your right hand.

81

Fig.2 *Kosadachi*. Bend your knees and look to your right.

❶

Fig.3 Left arm: *Fumikomi;* right arm: *Kakeuke.* Make a stamp kick with your right foot and right open hand block.

Fig.4 Make a left elbow strike.

❸

❹

Fig.5 Pull both hands to your right side. Look to your left.

Fig.6 Make a downward block with your left hand.

❺

❻

Fig.7 *Kagizuki.* Make a hook punch with your right hand.

85

Fig.8 *Kosadachi.* Move your right foot to cross over your left foot.

❼

Fig.9 Make a stamp kick with your left foot and inside block with your left hand.

⑧

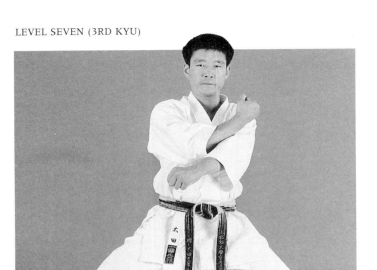

Fig.10 Left arm: *Nagashiuke*; right arm: *Gedanuke*. Make a downward block with your right and an upper block with your left hand.

Fig.11 Make a back fist strike with your left hand.

❾

❿

Fig.12 Look to your left.

Fig.13 Left arm: *Namigaeshi*; right arm: *Sokumenuke*. Pull your left foot up quickly towards your right thigh, and make a block with your left hand, your right fist under your left elbow.

⓬
Fig.14 Look to your right.

Fig.15 Pull your right foot up quickly towards your left thigh, and make a block with your left hand, with your right fist under your left elbow.

Fig.16 Pull both hands to your right hip and look to your left.

Fig.17 Left arm: *Chudanzuki*; right arm: *Kagizuki*. Make an attack to your left with left hand punch and right hand hook punch with *Kiai*.

Fig.18 Cross both arms and make an open hand attack to your left.

Fig.19 Make a right elbow strike.

17

18

Fig.20 Pull both hands to your left hip and look to your right.

95

Fig.21 Make a down-ward block with your right hand.

❶❾

❷⓿
Fig.22 Make a hook punch with your left hand.

Fig.23 *Right.* Cross your left foot over your right foot.

Fig.24 *Below.* Make a stamp kick with your right foot and inside block with your left hand.

97

Fig.25 Make a downward block with your left hand and upper block with your right hand.

Fig.26 Make a back fist strike with your right hand.

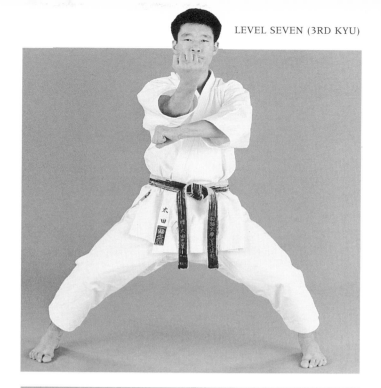

㉓

Fig.27 Look to your right.

㉔

Fig.28 Pull your right foot quickly up towards your thigh, and make a block with your right hand, your left fist under your right elbow.

Fig.29 Look to your left.

Fig.30 Pull your left foot quickly up towards your thigh, and make a block with your right hand, your left fist under your right elbow.

27

102

Fig.31 *Above.* Pull both hands to your left side. Look to your right.

Fig.32 *Above, right.* Make an attack to your right with right hand punch and left hand hook punch with *Kiai*.

Fig.33 Move your right foot back to your left foot to ready position.

Application

Figs 34, 35, 36 and 37 show the application of figs 28 to 32.

Fig.34

Fig.35

Fig.36

Fig.37

Kumite: one-step sparring

As in Level six, but to include roundhouse kick.

Levels eight/nine/ten
(2nd kyu/1st kyu/1st Dan)

Kihon

Combinations of all previous basic techniques.

Kata: bassai dai

Fig.1 *Yoi* (ready). Move your right foot to your left foot and cover your right fist with your left hand.

Fig.2 *Soeteuke*. Stamp with your right foot and make a block with your right hand, your left hand open to support your right wrist.

❶

Fig.3 Move your left foot to your rear. Make a left hand inside block.

Side view

Fig.3

❷

Side view

Fig.4 *Uchiuke*. Make an inside block with your right hand.

Side view

Fig.4

❸

Side view

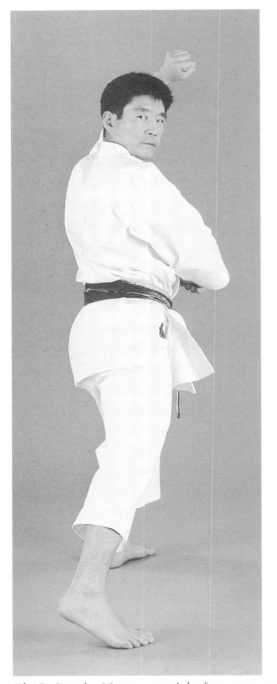 

Fig.5 *Sotouke*. Move your right foot, turn to your rear and make a left hand outside block. ❹

Fig.6 Make an inside block with your right hand. ❺

Fig.7 Right arm: *Gedansukuiuke*; left arm: *Sotouke*. Pull your right foot back to your left foot. At the same time swing your right arm in a downward movement and continue to step forward and make an outside block with your right hand.

Fig.7

❻

❼
Fig.8 Make an inside
block with your left hand.

Fig.9 Move your left foot and pull both hands to your right side.

❽

Fig.10 Left arm: *Tateshutouke*. Make an open hand block with your left hand to a ❾ position in front of your left shoulder.

Fig.11 Make a straight punch with your right hand.

Fig.12 *Below, left and right.* Twist your hip to the side and make an inside block with your right hand.

Fig.13 Make a straight punch with your left hand.

Fig.14 *Below, left and right*. Twist your hip and make an inside block with your left hand.

Fig.15 Step forward and make a right knife hand block.

Fig.16 *Below, left.* Step forward and make a left knife hand block.

Fig.17 *Below, centre.* Step forward and make a right knife hand block.

Fig.18 *Below, right.* Step back and make a left knife hand block.

Fig.19 *Tsukamiuke*. Shift your weight to your left foot and make a circular block with your right hand as if to grab your opponent's arm, with your left hand supporting your right wrist.

Fig.20 Left arm: *Tsukamiyose*; right arm: *Gedankekomi*. Bring your right knee up between your arms and make a downward thrust kick, pulling your hands up towards your chest, with *Kiai*.

Side view

Side view

⓳

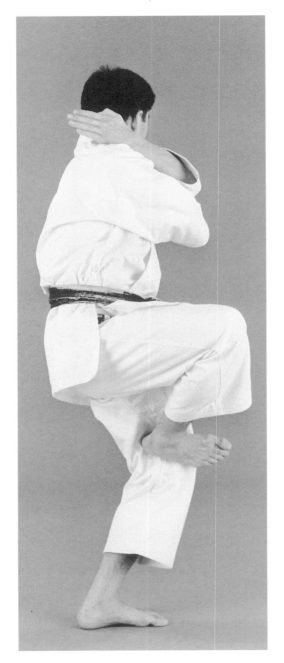

Fig.21 Step with your right foot to make a left knife hand block.

Side view

Fig.21

Side view

Fig.22 Step forward and make a right knife hand block.

Side view

Fig.23 *Morotejodanuke*. Pull your right foot back to your left and make a double hand upper rising block.

Side view

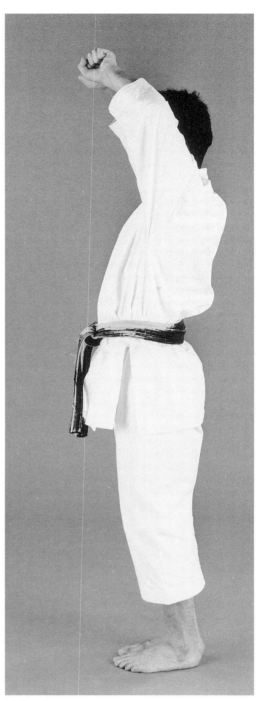

Fig.23      Side view

Fig.24 *Kantsuihasamiuchi*. Pull your hands apart and step with your right foot to make a circular strike with both hands to your opponent's mid-section.

Side view

Fig.25 Slide forward and make a punch with your right hand.

Fig.26 Left arm: *Nagashiuke*; right arm: *Gedanuchikomi*. Move your left foot and turn to your rear. Make an open hand block with your left hand and a downward knife hand strike with your right hand.

Fig.27 Left arm: *Gedanuke*; right arm: *Jodanuchiuke*. Pull your left foot to
your right into a back stance, and make an upper inside block with your
right hand and a lower downward block with your left hand.

㉕

Fig.28 Make a stamp kick with your right foot into a straddle stance, and make a downward block with your right hand to your left side. ㉖

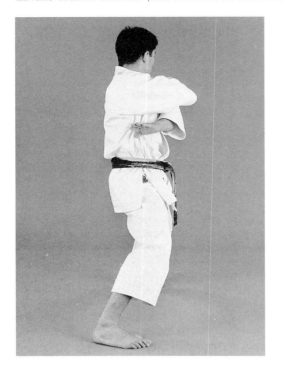

Fig.29 *Kakeuke*. Look to your left, cross your arms (left under right) and make an open hand block with your left hand to your left side.

Side view

Fig.30 Left arm: *Mikazukigeri*; right arm: *Empi*. Make a crescent kick with your right foot to your left hand.

Side view

Fig.31 Make a right elbow strike.

Side view

Fig.32 Make a right downward block with your right hand, your left fist against your right elbow.

Side view

Fig.33 Make a down-
ward block with your left
hand, your right fist
against your left elbow.

Side view

Fig.34 *Gedanuke*. Make a downward block with your right hand, your left fist against your right elbow.

Side view

141

Fig.35 Look to your right. Pull both hands to your left side and shift your weight to your right foot towards a front stance.

Side view

Fig.36 *Yamazuki.* Make a 'U' punch to your opponent's face and mid-section with your left and right hands.

Side view

Fig.37 Pull your right foot back to your left foot, and both hands to your right side.

Side view

Fig.38 Lift your left knee and make a 'U' punch to your opponent's face and mid-section with your right and left hands.

Side view

Fig.38

Side view

Fig.39 Pull your left foot back to your right, both hands to your left side.

Side view

Fig.40 Lift your right knee, step forward and make a 'U' punch to your opponent's face and mid-section with your left and right hands.

Side view

Side view

Fig.41 *Sukuiuke*. Pivot on your right foot and move your left foot to your left side. Make a downward sweeping block with your right hand.

Fig.42 Shift your weight to your right knee and make a downward sweeping block with your left hand.

Fig.43 Pull your left foot halfway and step with your right foot to make a 45° ㊵
knife hand block with your right hand.

Fig.44 Keeping your hands in position, slowly move your right foot to make a right knife hand block position, at the same time looking over your left shoulder.

41

㊷

Fig.45 *Above.* Pull your right foot about halfway towards your left foot and step with your left foot to make a left knife hand block with *Kiai*.

Fig.46 Pull your left foot back to your right to the ready position.

Application

Fig.47 Shows the application of fig.7.

Fig.48 shows the application of fig.20.

Fig.49 shows the application of fig.39.

Jiyu ippon kumite:
semi-free one-step sparring

For semi-free one-step sparring, both opponents adopt a free style position. Both attacker and defender can move about freely. The attacks are pre-arranged, and the defender can make any block and counter attack.

Glossary

PUNCHING TECHNIQUES
Chudan junzuki: stepping punch to the stomach
Empi: elbow strike
Gyaku zuki: reverse punch
Jodan junzuki: stepping punch to the face
Kentsuiuchi: hammer fist strike
Nukite: spear hand strike
Shutouchi: knife hand strike
Uraken: back fist strike

BLOCKING TECHNIQUES
Age uke: rising block
Gedan barai: downward block
Shuto uke: knife hand block
Soto uke: outside block
Uchi uke: inside block

KICKING TECHNIQUES
Mae geri: front snap kick
Mawashi geri: round kick
Ushiro geri: back kick
Yoko geri keage: side snap kick
Yoko geri kekomi: side thrust kick

Chudan: stomach
Gedan: lower
Jodan: face

STANCES
Kiba dachi: straddle stance
Kokutsu dachi: back stance
Zenkutsu dachi: front stance

Dojo: training hall
Gi: karate suit
Kata: forms
Keri: kicking
Kihon: basic
Kumite: sparring
Makiwara: striking board
Seiken: fist
Tsuki: punching
Uchi: striking

Index